Rural, Rock'n the Ridiculous

by

Charles Measures

**Grosvenor House
Publishing Limited**

Charles Measures is hereby identified as author of this
work in accordance with Section 77 of the Copyright, Designs
and Patents Act 1988

The book cover picture is copyright to Charles Measures

This book is published by
Grosvenor House Publishing Ltd
28-30 High Street, Guildford, Surrey, GU1 3HY.
www.grosvenorhousepublishing.co.uk

A CIP record for this book
is available from the British Library

ISBN 1-905529-87-2

❧ Trust Me ❧

May I impose
my ego and genius
upon you ?
I am a poet.

You know you want me
to, really
I promise it won't hurt, to let me
under your skin.

I can always stop, when I have gone
too far
with the smooth seduction of my polished
words, revealing
insights we can share together,
from the open pages of my translated heart.

Who can resist
such subtleties of refinement,
pursued in every crafted phrase ?

Let the overtures in my rhyming schemes
be your escort,
as you take your place, to stand
in line, with the queue
forming around the block,
for the privilege of acquiring
one copy of my book.

Introducing Rural, Rock'n The Ridiculous

I have always had more than one style of writing poetry. This may be in part due to the fact that I was born in Lincolnshire, Tennyson's home county and yet my nick name was 'Frank', after Frank Zappa, the legendary U.S. avant-garde rock musician, who held some highly outspoken points of view. Consequently, one of my styles leans towards romantic and rural traditions, whilst the other is definitely more 'street' or Rock and Roll, if not at times off the wall. I realize this could be interpreted as forever falling between two stools, but that would be assuming that there were two stools there in the first place.

When taking part in poetry readings I would usually read a selection from three different folders: The Undertow, "Hand Me The Acoustic" and "Own Up. Who Wrote This?" The Undertow contained the personal and autobiographical poems, whereas "Hand Me The Acoustic" was predominately humourous. "Own Up..." meanwhile was for my right hook, or quizzical poems. The lack of beer bottles thrown through chicken wire, or caffe lattes poured down the back of my Earl Jean floral shirt suggest that during the course of an evening, I must have got the balance between these three folders right.

It therefore seemed natural when putting this collection together, to group the poems under the same folder headings. Whilst each section is self-contained, the reader can still alternate between these three very different sections, as if I was giving a reading myself.

The author admits wilful acts of ego on the rampage in the following contents:

The Undertow.

"Hand Me The Acoustic"

"Own Up. Who Wrote This?"

Beat The Critics.

The Undertow

"If you don't change the road you're on, you might end up getting there."

"Bad as you are, you know how to give good things to your children. How much more, will your Father in heaven give good things to those who ask him!"

Matthew 7 : 11

Introducing The Undertow

Lincolnshire's sidelined geographical position, in relation to much of the country, has allowed its landscape, which is naturally suited to agriculture, to retain its rural ways of life, customs and values, far longer than many other counties. However, within its borders it exhibits a dual personality. The charm of the picturesque sweep of the hills and valleys of the Wolds gives way, the further east one travels towards the coast, to the stark and exposed, flat expanse of the Fens, hemmed in by the North sea.

The author was born into this county way of life, amongst the large landowners of the gentry and the aristocracy, with their attendant boarding school and military traditions. Being the last left in the line, there was the family expectation to carry on the duties of a substantial farming estate, and a generation of successful horse racing. However the author was pulled between respecting the sense of family responsibilities he had been brought up with and his own natural inclinations to music and guitar playing. This was compounded further when the family moved permanently to the ancestral home in the Fens, which the author had always had grim forebodings about. These forebodings were not to go unfounded.

This background, with its resultant tragedies, and a resolve to determine a greater sense of destiny, is the underlying theme in the following sequence of poems.

❧ Groundsweat ❧

The clarity of the passing bell
recedes, like snowbones
in the groundsweat coating
upon the winter leaves.
The palms of cobwebs stretched,
across the barren pores of strangled
gorse.

As resolute,
as the blacksmith's hammered blows,
beside the furnace sparks,
the numbered years, in wrapped conclusion,
struck steady in its metered tongue:
heads lifting in the furrowed fields.
Cold eyed pennies placed beyond
the tollbar's reach.

Seasons turning round, within its wooden
cask, the grandfather clock stands,
guard upright, in its vigil beside the door.

The sentry's swinging march resounds
as footsteps across the hall, retiring
up the stairs.
The unhinged bag of superstition
disposed
at the wake-woman's practised craft.

～ Who's There? ～

The feet that walked away,
whatever words were said.
A foreign matter transferred,
contagion in the head.

A flight that was grounded,
a continent from home,
doctor's advice determined
to leave him on his own.

Answers he can't remember,
for questions too young to ask,
is he still their little boy,
after a year lost in the dark?

What if the nightmares surface?
Only time will tell.
Is there a god to call upon
and finally lift the spell?

✺ Little Boy B.Goode ✺

My musical prescription, repeated daily,
and self administered , as often as
required, after the bed of convalescence
and release from doctors' notes, recorded
in their thin white sleeves.

My first name labelled, on the remedial
track, to the backwoods' boy,
whose lack of formal learning
played right into his hands.

Two years late for the nursery bell,
the 3 'R's stacked against me, on my
deck of slow resolution,
stuck at speed 16,
and interests outside the r.p.m.
of regulated parental music, at 33:
no singular achievement of a topping
45, but the two 'R's of Rock and Roll
fast tracked to 78,
turning tables on the charts
and tips of monitored development.

The duck walk posture and miming
racquet swung low,
golloping in the evergreen
acres of Axe Minster carpet, towards
the photo opportunities in the window
panes' reflection, each glued
within their crittall frames.

The chugging rhythm of heartbeat
thriving, and the electric twang
of whistle blowing, from my train,
a long way down the line.

Mr Goode Be Gone

(The Gentry's View. Circa 1960)

Mr Goode,
unfortunately, an American,
from Louisiana, we pronounce 'our na'
as ' anna' would be the wrong side
of the castle keep, granting access
to the grounds of the estate.

Mr Goode,
a guitar strummer and purveyor
of box car culture, a perceived threat
to the diction of refinement,
lowering the tone of propriety and
deportment in the seats of country
piles.

~ Wild West Stage ~

Stand up,
to the bull barrelled bluff,
and lamp dark
closing
down the foresight
in the field.

Surrounded
by make believe
within
the clearing
for undertaking showdowns,
reflection is still
the dead
giveaway, an involuntary
glint that toys
from the hideout, beyond
the black stump
hollow.

No need to count
up to 200
paces
to come alive
again,
or demean
the lowest calibre of chicken
run behind
the impatient creak of the barn
door's swing.

Polish off
the smear of menace
and prove the trust
in stopping power.

Above the fireplace
hangs
the centre piece,
a history
of black powder
and sooted initials,
from bygone campfire talk:
a forged engraving, etched
into the sturdy stock,
threatening
to call you
out:

the son of a gun.

Valentine

If I had words to speak,
what secrets could I tell,
in the safety of the playground
before the classroom bell?

It was in the way I saw you,
I could not understand,
why peace was an undiscovered word,
you slipped into my hand.

If curls and ribbon will guard this time
and bridge the river flow,
I choose you to remember me,
where ever I must go.

What presents can I offer,
but all my prayers for you?
Will time deny the asking,
one kiss,
to make a dream come true?

❧ Unquestioned ❧

A flotilla of white puff clouds
slowly
absorbs to grey, in the winter's cut,
on the far horizon.

A school boy straggle engages
in its Sunday troop,
the afternoon conscription of the gangly
crocodile.

No Garden of England this, but Thanet,
Isle of cabbage patches and bungalows.

How many regiments, like us,
this day will pass,
marching out their terms of duty,
backbone built in the tradition,
that sends away to school?

And when the orders come,
in later years, will we then ask
"why?"
we are stranded in some foreign field
and left, this time
to die?

❧ "San Francisco Calling." ❧

In the summer of 1967 dog fights were re-enacted over the skies of Kent, for a major film production on the Battle Of Britain. This proved a welcome distraction for many school boys from their outdoor activities.

Against the back drop of wide-angled sky,
sights re-align
on dog fight displays, peppering
mid air theatre, staged
above the bowler's arm of hostile delivery
and parried defense
driving beyond the boundary covers.

A blockbuster re-enactment and grandstand
preview
for white flannelled boys and staff,
patrolling the afternoon slog,
through the season's declaration of matches
and practice nets.

Heads lift in remembrance,
to the dare devil few, who grounded
their belief, to be forever England,
in the smear of smoke and tracer, daubed
into the canvas of the Kentish sky.

And thus provide unexpected
animation for the Airfix kits, drying
amongst the tins of Humbrol paint:
wings and fuselages awaiting
assembly, on the window ledges:
a hobby deemed appropriate for pursuits
in leisure time.

I signed up, my commitment
to "The Burning Of The Midnight Lamp".
Its wong wong sound and healthy volume
a bouncing bomb of boom
confusing birdsong and overwhelming masters
tapping pipes,
in the sanctity of the common room's discharge.

A radio transmitting,
"Hi there! San Francisco calling.
Make love, not war."

If not far out, most
certainly removed,
to the art school, dropping
paint on psychedelics, defined
where I was at:

a one way trip, keeping 'right on'
down the corridor to the Headman's
negative wave.
My peace dictated with fingered gestures,
as he walked in and turned
a whiter shade of pale.

⟶⟞ The Stake ⟝⟵

Each morning, from the 'Big House'
the Gaffer's son strode out
to the potato gangs, across the fields:
the fourteen year old 'casual',
with a hereditary interest,
'as far as the eye could see.'

The 'Young Un' could keep up:
the boarding school outsider,
amongst the Lincolnshire dialect and
softened German accents, rooted resolutely
in the validity of the family name:
honouring the season's rite of backs bent
in homage to the earth.

The cyclical rhythm of arms filling basket
after wicker basket, left positioned,
like miniature tank traps, fortifying
the field against some invisible 'haar'
that would breach
the token gesture of solitary trees,
stationed,
between the low level defence of hedges and proliferation
of shrub, surrounded,
by the cold indifference of the Wash,
ally to Siberian winds from the Russian Steppes,
that would sweep the marshes and flatlands of the Fen,
deep into the submersion of its winter retreat.

The invigilation of the sun, posted
in its summer command,
flanked potato sacks, sand-bagged high,
at 11 o'clock,
temporary cover for rounds of sandwiches
and gum.

This was peace, their settled home
amongst the trial of elemental combat:
their blood price,
beyond the years of trench-fill
from industrial slaughter
and the measled rash of swastika,
plaguing the continental landscape.

Their peace amongst themselves:
the carpenter, walking slowly,
deceived by the dawn of man- made mist
encroaching
over the stumps of No Man's Land:
former P.O.W.s, based around the strips,
from which the bombers lumbered,
in their nocturnal course,
dropping sleek translations of 'land reclamation.'

He sensed the pull to fathom
the claim of earth staked through him
and all he knew.

One night, whilst he slept,
fast as a church,
the water would blanket all.
Darkness would be laid to rest
upon the surface of the deep,
as it was ….in the beginning.

≈ Style ≈

It was an unexpected accolade,
as unexpected, as the onslaught
upon my father's sight and parishioners
in their Sunday best:

a phosphorescent vibrancy that required.....
shades
for all whose glances stole upon
this apparition, modelling
the finest definition of Kings road
hip, imported
to the village church.

The proud exuberance of orange,
brightly captured
in a shirt, overflowing
across the jacket, in a cavalier
declaration of ruffles and ornamented
frills, that drove
the rump of cavalry twills and hounds-tooth
to the furthest outpost of the regimented
pews.

"Boy, that's a horrible shirt."

⚜ The Night Watch ⚜

If I held your hand, or kissed your lips,
you would know no more
than the breath of moonbeams,
and the fingertips of midnight
weaving
the curtain-sail of dreams,
along the shoreline of your hair.

Under the spell of petals floating
promises and the whispers
of my prayer,
keep sake the charm of wishes,
from your roof top to the sky.

The rosary of your name
echoes
softly on the air.

☙ Her House ❧

I. Re-visited

It took a short walk from her house,
to the churchyard,
but once
much longer to say goodbye.

     ……………………………

Through the garden gate,
as ever, still open
the path lingered,
along a composition of timeless perfection:
the shawl of roses and touch of scent,
a cradle of hedge around the lawn.

The unfinished flower bed, only the earth
newly turned.

Relevant details had been laid out in the papers.
'For sale' put into the ground.

Paint peeled,
tiles were slipping
over a bare frame of timbers.

Wallpaper tears, with no warmth to retain,
exposed an ugly gash of plaster.
Fingers of damp slowly smothered.

     ……………………………

Two days after Ascension,
which she had marked with her devotion,
her father saw her,
from the ladder he had placed
against her bedroom window:
motionless,
still ever seeing,
the flesh embodiment of a stone angel.

A physical presence,
flawless in the craftman's touch,
yet severed from the burden of importune.
Life no longer conceived
as returning,
raw material dispersed to dust,
upon the workshop floor.

There had been no thief in the night,
for a house
filled with so much peace.
She had always known where she was going,
if not so soon,

as did her friends:
a bewildered congregation
of bright young things and twenty-somethings,
who scarcely had an item of black among them,
except for Balls and social occasions.

But she would have understood.
She too was wearing her favourite dress.

🦢 II. Funeral Prayer 🦢

Forgiveness,
to whom should it be given,
in this,
the final prayer?

The witness of my buried heart
still breaking,
from spoken words undone.

The seizure
of this break of bells, struck
down upon
your day of vows, that would never
bind in blessing
round the trail of gown,
or sweep further
than the wraps of bloom, sprung
shivering, with the late fall
soil.

The strength
in ever parting chords, to be
plucked
across the strings of my guitar,
remain
as unconfessed, as the harmony
transposed,
in your chosen song,
to stay, "Forever
Young"
and now you always
would.

I still wish
I could have kissed you
just one more time.

❧ A Window Opens ❧

Can the wash of colour reduce
the face of the infinite,
stretched across a canvas frame,

or the flow of words compress
the truth, between the lines
on an empty page?

A window opens
onto meadows and the longstanding
distance.

Animals move
steadily
under the rainbow's arc.

❧ Handed Down ❧

I. A Choice Of Weapon

It was a hip term of ritual significance,
professed
after a tribal gathering at a "prog" rock concert,
or the first hearing of a concept album,
offering
organic ego development from an extra terrestrial
planet of confused commercial
hedonism.

"Hey man! That really blew my mind."

My father, though a farmer, never 'dug'
'the deep' sounds of the soul,
or cross fertilisation of ethnic rhythms
into western culture.

'Really deep' – was for carcasses
in the earth
and 'depth' – only so much
as seeds would germinate
in the soil.

He marvelled that my 'axe'
cost as much
as his favoured weapons of destruction,
a pair of Purdeys, handed down.

Yet a generation apart,
it was still the same blood
that ran down fingers
onto tuning pegs and steel strings
or fencing posts and barbed wire
strands.

The same blood tied to the land,
the tradition that was
as it is now
and always will be.
You can do what you want
as long as you answer to me.

"The camouflaged uniform is the perfect disguise,
to be in a group and shoot life from the skies.
Check out these tweeds and life is complete,
your hair is too long, when you march to our beat."

From the devouring auditorium within a corn dryer's
isolation,
an attack of amplified notes
pierced
the unrelenting stretch of Fenland sky,
fleeing with the birds,
escaping the trajectory of pellets
and confines of the county.

Yet he blew his mind,
a few yards only, but enough
to separate mind from soul,
and dribble
down the grassy slope,
into the deep
trough of the rain filled
ditch.

The spotlight was late for the final act,
12 – 14 hours before
the car headlights pinned down
the body of copy
for the local
news,
and a further four until the trickle
of condolences arrived, with the startled
jolt
of early morning milk crates.

Something snapped as inevitable
as an amplifier switched on,
or a safety catch clicked off.
The flow of cash and blood dried up.

≈ II. A Family Tradition ≈

My father and his before
knew when to put an animal down
and practised what they preached
on themselves;
keeping the family tradition
good shots to the end.

⊰ III. Who Called The Shots? ⊱

Once was circumstantial, but twice
was not by chance:
the silent witness of a distant
presence watching

the final drive and committed walk,
to the remotest edge, in the furthest
field.

The same ritual, fifteen years apart,
discharging
determined desperation and honour.

Had they traded more than crops
or horses,
at some crossroads
further back in time,
before each son was born, to carry
on the line?

Had the darkest shadow of Yourself
come to call
collect
the price
one favoured cartridge
each
chosen for a quick dispatch?

Death favours reliability.

In Your own words, tell me,
was there anything they said,
some contrite word from self-made men,
before they took it on the chin?

Did they believe
they were in Your place
and their sacrifice of blood
destroy
the false idols in their souls
which You had cursed as sin?

❧ IV. Good Friday Agreement ❧

An accidental opportunity, to take
out,
what my father had not foreseen:

the ghost of Peter
in denial, with the cock crow's
accusations.

This apostate's vision blunted, beyond
preserving
the barrel length of his gun
and self
possessed lumber, within
the exposed flank of the field,
where the elements
had mashed
my father's ashes with the nutrients
in the soil.

The trophy of his bulk, asking
to be collected, across
the sheer front of the bull
bar's frame.

See the arms
outstretched.

Those hands
straight
upon the wheel, and count
the price of nails.

❧ V. Bloodline ❧

Guilty. Collusion

in the need for blood and reconciliation
that flowed down generations,
along the Roman spear
on what was just another Friday afternoon
detachment,
until the weekend detail dispersed,
scouting for bodies.

One generation surveying
where his father's body had been
removed from the land,
prepared for a new season,
gauged with plough and scarred
with harrow.

One generation down, the last
left in the line
reviewed foreclosure demands
served lately on his father;
confirmation lying
in the mortuary, with the family
likeness blown away.

God arrived.
He had come for his Boy.
There would be hell to pay
and this time, it was personal.
Very personal.

✎ Grey Sovereign ✎

In 1964, Jack Measures, a successful race horse owner, sold the stallion Grey Sovereign for £100,000. In 1981, The London Community Gospel Choir, England's first mainstream gospel choir, formed as a result of the Brixton riots.

My natural polemic, predisposed
to Rolling Stone,
counter-cultural alternative to the
Farmers' Weekly,
(Heavy Rock versus Big Tackle),
did not qualify my street credentials
to pass out,
along the highway of staging posts,
from the windy city to the Santa Monica
boulevards, guitars and amps
fully loaded on the Kenworth truck
of dreams: rolling my dice
on Route 66.

My grandfather's tailored showcase,
top hat and binoculars, prominent
in the royal stand,
spurring on the bloodstock prices
beyond the champagne and lather,
foaming at the winner's post.
In lieu of debts, he played
his cards, and took the horse;
his social ascent mounting,
from the Croft Marsh turf, to Ascot's
firmer going of the sport of kings.

From the Pilgrim Fathers' east,
the Ford Capri of destiny swung
to Leytonstone via Knightsbridge:
the A-Z of tight grids and urban sprawl
transposing over the spread of coastal
plain and transverse sections of waterways.
The SW7 refugee adrift
from the raft of executors and family estate

vanishing
in a tide of liquidation, and smoke
of fat cigars, incorporated in the black
hole of county bank.

Oxford-English reserve meets laid back
Afro-Caribbean cool, welded
beyond the summer flames of east
end barricades and burning cars:
the final fire watch along the blackened
fields, embers of the family harvest
home. Day to day living forging
Unity, "Out of many people, the faith of one,
true voice": the dynamics of gospel rhythm
and wings of vocal soul.

A creative heart and administrative head
to dot the " I s" and cross the " T s"
of logistics,
for a pioneering army of young
ambassadors striking
out from their communities' suspicion,
of racial harmony and cultural goodwill.

From Ulster's quagmire of sectarian
divide,
to the limo-ed poodle perms strutting
anthems in the shrines of arena rock,
and liberating
the protocol behind the freshly painted
boxes, at the bow of the royal command;
respect translated into the new
heritage of "Gospel Greats" burgeoning,
in the Christmas racks and celebrations
of association awards.

My grandfather's tips on form and music
never prejudiced my ears, but imbued
a faith, to leave
a running legacy, beyond
the Sovereign years.

He was open for business,
"There's no such thing as a married man,
a hundred miles from home."

He traded guitar licks
for those he craved around his talent,
from the women who kept him hard.

Each performance scheduled
between the nightly convoy of trucking
that rolled
around the procession of outstretched hands
into the coral,
to receive the ceremonial communion of primeval
rhythm.

Keeping an eye on the mirror,
he believed
in his own name
that what he saw was good.

A high priest of sacrifices, dedicated
to the road,
as devoid of meaning as the wedding ring
hidden in countless sets of custom
guitar strings, discarded every night.

He had what it took
to suck and f... his way
up to the top.

❧ Rich Running ❧

Thorough-bred icons:
acquired from performance related bonuses;
track records of the drive to succeed
and keeping the shareholders happy.

Engines remain idle,
until the steady procession from private roads,
on Saturdays, to the High street,
between 10 – 4 , the respected hours
for designer shopping.

A parade of custom colours and personalized
interiors, uniformly parked in
"Members Only".
The boasted conversations, across the bar,
of envied statistics, attributed to each model
of coveted chassis and glossy bodywork.

After the match,
the self-conscious grunt of acceleration
from the school gates, that dissipates
into the restriction of the 30 mile limit.
Baffled school boys watch the run-around
of their dream machines, from Blue-tack
clutching onto study walls and the regulation
overlap of pole position
pin ups.

Have they discovered the irony of success?
"Please sir,
to be married to Marilyn Monroe,
with no greater expectation
than a good night kiss."

❧ Storyboards ❧

(From An Early Childhood Illness)
I. White Wash

No fear of lion, or madman
certifying
the long case hours of days'
broad light,

and yet,
to whom do they belong?

Calendar dates scored through,
with binding underhand, involuntary
restraint on steps, to get
outside.

Sweetened treasons in the cradle speak
of bandages unfurling and white wash
slipping from the memory slate:
flesh upon the apparition, if belief
is to be possessed.

⚜ II. The Unanswered Prayer ⚜

Your word is spoken and it is done.
Your child cries out, "Thy kingdom come."

Your Son bows down. You turn your back.
"Why have you forsaken me?"
The sky turns black.

The ward is dark, "Thy will be done."
The child who screams will not live long.

☙ III. The Children's Ward ❧

Brooding shadows of flesh,
or light caress of ghost?
One does not move
with what the eye beholds, or mind conjures
in the murmurs of blacker darkness.

The horror of measured steps
on silent floor.

Who have they come for,
these silhouettes of practised drill,
that leave no trace and beds empty?

Shutters locking aperture.
Selection in the torchlight's beam.

Breathe
above a whisper, they can hear,
diverted from their purpose, they hover,
calculating
the hand of mercy or push into the void.

❧ IV. The Apple Picker ❧

The touch of presence:
a stifled rumour of submission,
to murmur under-breath,
intruding
in the half-light of your shadow.

The dark practice:
arms outstretched, apples snapped
from branch to branch,
beyond each passive blink,
unquestioned, in your naked eye.

The blindfold buff of imprint:
a squat of refugees groping
through the blackout, imposed
within the walls, inside
the orchard of your destiny.

"This wither of male supremacy
betraying the wraith of a distant master race.
Reconciliation blessed, beyond the terms
of peace, with fair hair and blue eyes."

The hanged gallows drop to memory:
startled murder of crows and ambush
of tigers treading
humiliation in the ruins of defeat.

Defences over whelmed in a pincer
movement penetrating
through the front and rear.
A cursed liberation,
releasing the flow of blood
and the union of hate,
to the seedbed's tortured sanctuary.

The bolt of terminal withdrawal:
gut in the nail claw, slice
of burial womb, stretchered in
the sluice of back street dirt
and brick:

the barren allegiance
of the right arm's salute
swung high.

✺ A Lightning Thought ✺

The kick drum of air turbulence and tantrums
of thunder sound
checking round the metalled out flight-case
suspended, above
the long distant drop, to the cymbals
crash of breaking waves.

The eco friendly crusader, unrecognised
by the elements, charging solo
along the world's meridian lines,
GMT, MTV :
keeping up the day job, the top
Dollar stadium draw.

The ultimate career move ready
to spark, mid air,
like the pyrotechnic finale,
staged with calculated precision,
in the budget costings and overheads:
boxed sets and retrospectives rocketing
into the stratosphere, as his own
celebrity plummeted,
into legend and the halls of fame.

His status and earnings checked in, together
with the sunglasses in the basket, at the security
scan of life, would not save him,
or pull the strings to extend the schedule
run, by popular demand,

or allow me, to attach my rider,
sitting across the aisle.

‏⁓ **The Narrator** ⁓

A week-end festival of arts and entertainment,
with late night theatre
drawing Friday to a close.
I should have seen dance and drama,
but all I saw was you.

Was it the role you were playing,
or the gift of your personality,
portrayed in your character
that made me stare,
beyond the crinolines of your costume
into the heart of your performance,
that never left my eyes?

Notes and flowers were left, at back stage doors,
with sympathetic doormen, as we missed each other
a day or two apart
from the same venue, on separate tours.

During an escalating summer
of concert halls and studios,
each performance gathered its own momentum,
as I collected programmes and headlines
for future memories,
in the secret hope of children.

Spring snow captured
time and hearts, long enough
to settle two futures
and place my ring upon your finger.

One afternoon, whilst swimming,
the water receded
down the long stream of your hair,
across the lower reaches of your back,
to discover the black outline of
your swimsuit.

If time ever stood still,
or heaven caught its breath,
it was then
when I saw you,
climbing out of the water:

the brush stokes of infinite symmetry
drawing
the deep sigh of unspoken words,
across the pallet of graceful
poise
and confident fulfillment:
the glaze of pronounced beauty,
caressed into flesh.

As when,
Adam first saw Eve
and melted in disbelief
to still feel her breath upon his face
and know he was not dreaming.

The assurance of her being, within
time and word, conceived
the hint of an everlasting
truth, a permanent
desire to bless.

The mysteries of silence
confiding
within a whispered
touch.

"Hand Me The Acoustic."

Introducing "Hand Me The Acoustic."

Those of you with long memories, and in all probability large record collections, will remember in the 60's and the 70's when it was mandatory for every heavy rock group to get in touch with their feminine side and record an acoustic track for each L.P release, that bore no resemblance to what was on the rest of the album. It was, however, useful if your parents unexpectedly returned to the house after you had cranked up the Hi-Fi. All that was needed was to switch to afore mentioned acoustic track and your parents perception of your good taste and discernment would be instantly affirmed.

Look on this collection of my poems as a selection of acoustic tracks, with the indulgence of a heavy rock solo thrown in every so often. If you would like to see some of my more 'seriously deep' poems: irony, bathos, naked ambition (or the lack of any ambition), the dualism of personality and identity in the isolation of 21st century nepotistic culture, (you know the sort of thing), please ask for one of my maximum intensity folders.

May you always run bare foot through the grass, man.

✒ Whose Are These? ✒

He was wearing clean underwear
on the day
he was run over by the bus.
Unfortunately,
they were pink;
a forgotten item
at the back of a drawer,
retrieved in an emergency,
when the tumble dryer packed up.

On regaining consciousness,
he could not remember
who he was.

The nursing staff,
having sufficiently recovered their composure,
with one flimsy clue to
"Go on"
began with gender issues.

"Coming out"
of hospital
would take on a whole new meaning.

❧ Culture Shock ❧

I was not expecting this,
life as I knew it coming to an end
at the crossroads, in the High street,
during the middle of the school run,
in Epsom,
market town of horse racing
and retired army colonels.

A pulsating tremor
vibrating through my 4 x 4
suggesting:
a stampede of elephants rampaging
through the town, in search of peanuts,
on limited offer, in jumbo buckets,
promoted by the Odeon:

the world's largest squadron of 747s
thundering, low level overhead
with Richard Branson, practising
fuel conservation:

the synchronetic collapse of the forest
of scaffolding outside Sony and Pizza Hut,
in sympathy with the pavement,
being trampled underfoot:

the final madness and crescendo,
before
the gong of oblivion.

The overwhelming feeling
that King Kong had crash- landed
behind my vehicle and was stomping
to the rhythm of a MotorHead track,
three days into its ending.

This repetitious thump
punching my seat into my back.
The mechanical permutations of my track
rod end being buried in the sump.

The menace of black tinted windows,
looming
in my rear-view mirror,
embedded in something
resembling a bat-mobile with serious
metal-fatigue.

Inside, some dude and his bitch
were slapping
the steering wheel, the dashboard
themselves, each other,
on their way to the weekly shop
for groceries.

Their hands too unsteady
from all those chilled vibes exploding,
in the bowels of their thunder-box,
to place a coin in the slot,
for a supermarket trolley.

～ A Directive Of Intent ～

Our intelligence confirms :
the inevitability of his return.

We have reviewed, chapter and verse,
his biographical details, retrieved
from the shelves of historical best sellers
and the minority appeal of cults.
A resume of missed opportunities:
life- long membership of the Magic Circle,
and a bright future in storm abatement.

We are chairing constructive, top level cabinet
meetings, with all joiners engaged in retail
furniture and unusual garden sculptures.

We are studying religiously
any honours graduates combining theology
with the practice of alternative medicine.

Our biometric data does not stretch
to infinity.
We have requisitioned the Turin Shroud
to test for DNA
and enhance the facial imprint.

Forensics are dusting artefacts and scrolls
for the durability
of any latent force from the last time
he took off, allegedly vanishing
in a cloud of on- lookers hallucinations.

We understand how these things work:
the groundswell of good intentions and
informed curiosity that escalates
into public disorder,
upsetting the phylacteries of our respectable
citizens, for whom time is money.

Twice a year, they subscribe,
in the ballot plate of Christmas and Easter
offerings, to keep religion safe.

There will be no need for charges,
next time he returns,
or man hours tied-up corroborating
inconsistent statements of eye witness reports:
CCTV, in every market square; discreetly
camouflaged by any waters, renowned for fishing:
all footage admissible as evidence,
in secret.
The camera never lies.

The custom of a public hearing
deferred.
We merely suspect his words
conflict with our unequivocal belief
that all truth is relative
to the tolerance of religious equality, defined
within the constraints of oratorical propriety

But we will go easy on him,
no need for all that torture and mutilation.
Stoic martyrs, in their refusal
to let conviction die, can mislead our people's thought
to questions of eternal consequence
that lay bare to scrutiny
the unimpeachable source of our established
rule of law.

We would prefer an indefinite spell,
in solitary,
away from viewers casting lots,
"I'm the Son of God. Get me out of here."
until He has reformed
His theological ideals, within
our parameters of expectation
and then, perhaps, we might
all believe.

❦ Bounce ❧

Trampoline woman,
you have given new definition
to the word "bounce":
topless in your bikini bottoms,
lifting mid air,
serenely,
above my garden fence.

❧ Jessica Jane ❧

(The perils of driving past a lingerie shop in Esher on a Sunday)

It could have been so different,
if I'd turned the other way,
but the light was red
and when I saw you,
you had a great deal on display.

I should have seen it coming,
I would look once more,
so now I must protect you,
against those other men,
who stand staring at your door.

We have concluded an arrangement,
business is strictly best,
you have got my number,
I know your address.
You're discreet about my preference
for those items on your skin.
There's never anyone watching
on those days when I walk in.

Jessica Jane, you've trapped me
with your beauty and your cunning;
the promised rush of expectation
in what my eyes find stunning.
This cannot last forever,
because if my woman knows,
would she still want the gifts I buy her
to be worn underneath her clothes?

I don't know how to tell you,
this affair has gone too far,
I should be on the way to church
but now I've stopped the car.
Shall I sing Hallelujah,
or should I call your name?

Lord keep us from temptation
in the shape of Jessica Jane.

The Proverbial Thoughts Of A Father
On
Babies And Young Children

When women have babies, men acquire new Hi-Fi systems and then develop guilt complexes, in case they spend more time listening to the Hi-Fi than they spend with the baby.

When your wife comes home from hospital, having given birth, do not start watching Desperate Housewives, or re-runs of Bay Watch.

After a bottle feed, the still voice of calm is followed by the blower of the wind of change.

You find out who your friends are, when it is time to change a nappy.

When changing nappies, tights are a bummer.

Feeding solids to a baby with a cough is like playing Russian roulette with a muck spreader.

Nothing can prepare you for the horror of a baby being sick down the inside of your shirt.
It is even worse when you recognise what meal it is.
A wise son refrains from asking "Daddy, is it still warm ?"

A double buggy with tyre slashers clears the pavement.

A mother-in law does not know all there is to being a father.

The sign of successful baby/parent bonding is initiated by the baby sharing its innermost being with you. It snuggles up for a cuddle and then wipes its nose all over your newly washed pullover.

The effect of the word "poo" or "wee" uttered to a driver in the fast lane on a motorway, is the same as hearing England are losing 1-0 to the Faroe Islands in a World Cup qualifier.

The father who wears designer suits and carries twins, is like the man who clean his Ferrari by a rookery.

The Keynesian Economic Theory of Supply and Demand is illustrated by the example of the more ice cream you supply your children with, the more loo paper they will demand later on.

Blessed is the man who has many children when shopping at Tesco's; they fill their pockets with all manners of items at 100% discount prices.

The child who picks his nose is not welcome in the delicatessens of Guildford.

A young son who likes Ferraris is an invaluable ally against your wife's wishes to buy a Volvo estate.

Never sit in a dark room with a lava light, listening to the Grateful Dead and the baby intercom switched on, all at the same time.

You know a child has reached an understanding of finance, when he has saved his pocket money and declares" I won't spend my money today, I'll spend Daddy's instead."

All young children are geniuses with a paintbrush. If left unattended they can create a mural in the style of Jackson Pollock on your living room wall in a matter of minutes.

The son who says "Daddy, I'll buy you a Ferrari.......when I've discovered where Mummy keeps her money." has the keys to the Cosmos.

A parent's love should be as limitless as the number of times your offspring throw things from their high chair for you to pick up.

When a child has used up all his excuses as to why he should not go to bed, he will suddenly become riveted by Jeremy Paxman discussing the Gross National Product of Belgium.

❧ Twinned With? ❧

Time-capsuled, at first
under the sea,
a coastal Brigadoon with high profile
situations, to be filled
by the vacant
standard of the local rock hard:
"Fire watch for The Armada.
Knowledge of I-Spy and safety
matches essential."

Guess
where X marks the spot
of an architectural ruin, besieged
by the flatpack of a city,
which can conjure magic
with the name of Blodwyn Pig
headlining, to preserve
its cultural identity as a swinging place
for really big-shows?

Drive through, with loose change only
for the short stay
or else,
be prepared to lose
the will to live.

Domesticate Now

I love the smell
of my Morphy Richards
steaming,
first thing in the morning:

a round of ironing
to fully psyche me up
and celebrate the day.

An operations manual
to complete
a tour of duties
across the landing
sights of limbless action men,
and patrol the stockade
of the garden fence,
against incursions
from next door's little charlies.

The objective of my mission:
to clean up,
where no man has cleaned before.

❦ Q.E.D. ❧
(Quite Easily Dismissed.)

Question: What is the second greatest Commandment? Illustrate with an
example.

Answer: To love your neighbour,
As yourself,
Your fellow man who will spend
Eternity by your side.

Example: There is always one exception
That proves the rule,
Namely:

THE FRENCH.

COUNTRY AND WESTERN SINGERS.

VEGETARIANS.
(who never feed bones to their pet dogs).)

OWNERS OF CITROEN 2CVS
(who overtake you in the fast lane.)

ANYONE
(who phones when my wife is modelling her new lingerie)

MY DAUGHTER'S BOYFRIEND
(who drives a faster car than I do.)

MY OTHER DAUGHTER'S BOYFRIEND
(who earns more than I do.)

MY SON'S GIRLFRIEND
(who both drives a faster car and earns more than I do.)

RESULT: It all adds up
To one exception
That proves:
To pass the test
Never give your answer
Until you have fully understood
The question.

The following religious artefacts are offered for sale, with provenance: the sale to be divided into two sessions.

Old Testament Session.

Lots: Moses' Travel-Light Pyjama Case.

Toasted Manna Barbecue Set.

Elijah Firelighters.

Samson 2000 Hair Restorer.

City Of Jericho Planning Department's Regulations:

(For Bricklaying.)

New Testament Session.

Lots: The Observers Book Of Angels.

Lost Coin Detector.

Disciples Fishing Kit, With Speed Boat As Optional Extra.

Mint Condition Copy Of Judas Iscariot's Financial Guide:

" Money For Old Rope".

One Large Wooden Cross.
Auctioneer's Caveat:
> Personal Enquiries Only. This lot is believed to be cursed: bankrupted previous owner. Available for sale at a revelatory price.

ᴥ Can You Dig This? ᴥ

The poet offers the reader the chance to celebrate the true depth of poetic diversity, by choosing his, or her, choice of title, from the following selection, in a non judgmental way, which they believe best fits the meaning of the poem, should there be one:
Jamming / Losing It On The Road /
Where Was I At? / What Was I On? / Que?

So strung out, man,
with jamming.

The tail end swinging
its tight arrangement
to get on
down
the honky-tonking
paralysis,
tattooing that mean Hog's
Back.

The A3 section swelling
to 'slowissimo et
miserycordia,'
an original interpretation of an extended
improvisation, following
a road-works score.
The single bar line
riff of the Hook
repeating
harmonium Te Deum,
until transposed
into double
dead stop time.

The upfront horns, uptight,
Tooting question and response
to the bottle neck
sliding
non accelerando from the bridge,
to the fusion of pure country and south western bluegrass
flattened underfoot,

with the Wombles smoking in the woods
today, as they sample
those wild bunnies' Hip Hop
tracks.

The soft shoe tennis shuffle
smashing a delivery
of accidental agitato, down
into the grooves of Battersea's
urban bump and grind:
keep on pulling up,
to the bumper, baby,
in the middle of the road.

The hard bop downbeat
truncheon
tapping
do wop
in the Brixton streets.
Street cred knocking solid
citizens in un-Nike'd fashion. Changing
statements in the bling of an eye.
" Disgo here, and you go there"
into the ambient, solitary
agitato,
rapping vigoroso
behind the hard core slam.

The sunset licks
the crowding lighters of the stars
and the traffic lights test
positive, in eco friendly
green.

Man, this is hot.
Cooking
tyres shredding rubber,
laying it down
into the tarmac
on the road, still going
nowhere.

❧ The Main Attraction ❧

A thought provoking t- shirt,
boldly suggesting in black and white,
distinct anatomical impossibilities,
coupled with a chauvinistic desire for wish fulfillment.

The slogan still dozed
occasionally,
behind the boundaries of never- never land
in the fantasy studio of my mind:

a ceremonial ritual
celebrating
total immersion in chocolate,
presumably having been stripped
naked,
or left an hors d'oeuvres of minimal underwear,
before being thrown, or catapulted
by unspecified means, or persons unknown
to ....

where I was
          support act only
status, stranded between the stage
and the bar, to find it was
still working, after all
these years,
my animal magnetism, unconsciously
pulling the scores of women, to touching
preliminaries, admittedly
fully clothed,
but it wasn't that sort of gig.

Actually it was, if you were there
for the main attraction,
which I wasn't,
but I thought I was
the centre of attention,
as the extra curricular activities developed
out of hand,
with hands, in hands upon
some most particular places to go,

home for the finale of access all areas,
after the evening's encore
heightened the release of houselights and the focused
drift towards the catches snapping,
on the exit doors.

My totemistic stance
confounded the expectation of a cup of Horlicks,
or Bournvita in the kitchen,
let alone the chocolate spread upon
the table,
or wherever the preparations were to be applied.

My friends diagnosed, from their prescriptive
intake at the bar, and their paroxysms now
settled, that I was merely touched
by mental requisitions
cavorting on the make up couch,
beside the wardrobe door.
I wouldn't wear it well.

❧ Vinyl Man ❧
(at 50)

The Big 5 0 .
I actually made it.
A half century
of honours, awards ceremonies and
mass adulation.

In my dreams,
which I usually was,
but then again
no one else's.

All those column inches of tabloid
sensationalism,
I never filled:
kiss and tell exploits of three in a bed romps,
with super models
I wouldn't even recognize in the morning.

The network of celebrity contacts
I never made,
whilst schmoosing at private rehabs.
My agents's statement claiming it was
only exhaustion
and insisting I was still doing it
My Way:
sound bite portions, hacked
with alliteration
from the Gordon Ramsay school
of elocution, as to where
it all went
right
up.

At night
I inhale the incense of musky cardboard
sleeves,
peruse the straight lines of Blue Horizon,
Sun and Vertigo.
The rush

of week-end trips
to assembly halls and YMCAs
checking out consignments in wooden boxes:

Mint. 180G. Shrink-wrapped.

Deals done in cash.
Merchandise smuggled home
in brown paper and super market bags,
to be hoarded
in a massive stash of history.

I'm vinyl man.
Main man in the know
of what went down, with whom,
on independent labels of diversity
and the freedom to be progressive.

Custodian of the spinning plates
of Love, Peace and Revolution
decades
before marketing one size
fits all
reduced the product mix
to a conformity
in line with government directives
and political correctness.

The industry of human happiness
stifled
by advertisers' playlists programmed
in grey:
no perserverance needed
to reconcile black with white,
or the sacrifice of an artist's career.

"Keep America Beautiful. Get A Haircut."
the recruitment promise
to Vietnam Vets. And G.I.s
shorn like Samson of identity and respect
representing
the nightmare beauty of napalm
blossoming
over paddy fields and innocent civilians.

The tortured beauty of Star Spangled Banner
wrenched
from an ex- paratrooper's electric guitar,
defined the Woodstock generation
as their national dream
slid
into betrayal.

The unity of music with people
who marched
and the boys came home:
all races could take their place
and sit together, at least
in a bus.

Today
a new establishment of pop idols
and reality T.V.
Phone in gods
we will crucify in weeks,
with our vicarious craving to suck
in fame
and assert,
"We made you.
Be unto us, what we cannot do.
Create a life of meaning for ourselves."

Correspondence courses proliferate.
"Armchair Surgery" specialising in personality
dissection.
"Voyeurism." 24/ 7 . Cultivating that latent talent
to get it on in the jungle.
The fine art of binge drinking in designer clothes,
as someone discovers your X factor,
whilst propping up the bar.
All degrees of dumbing down.

Now old enough
to make both love and war,
I have kept the faith and never
sold out.

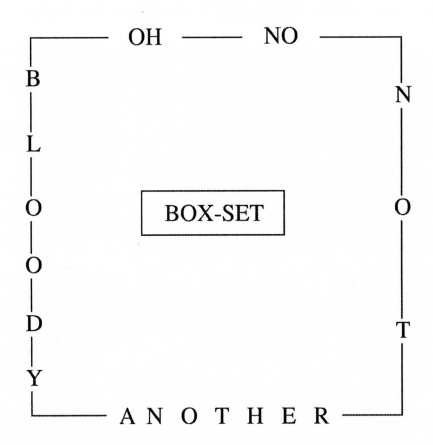

OH — NO

B
L
O
O
D
Y

BOX-SET

N
O
T

A N O T H E R

"Own Up.
Who Wrote This?"

Introducing "Own Up. Who wrote this?"

"Own up. Who wrote this?" was an expression I used when presented with a piece of music, which I either found incomprehensible, or felt compromised my musical integrity.

If you want to rock and get offered the musical equivalent of a "Walk through the Black Forest", then sometimes only a verbal right hook will do.

❧ Mid Life Soliloquy ❧

To be,
or have I been,
before a has been
becomes
what I am now ?

❧ Passion Wagon Blues ❧

In my younger days, of hormonal
imbalance,
I owned a passion wagon,
or at least,
the four wheeled side of the equation.

My mind, a confused
collision of figures and statistics,
overtook my senses, in pursuing
a motion of emergency legislation,
enforcing promiscuity as compulsory,
to be made retrospective,
to a date,
which had not worked out.

My M.P. understood, the premium
my policy would attract,
amongst the younger vote,
but his endorsements were not to be seduced
by party rights,
to stay up all night, and massage
votes in favor
of No, to Yes
and then abstain from all responsibility,
by falling asleep, behind
the wheel.

A Coiffure Too Far

Personally,
I have never been into
badgers' bottoms,
the hairstyles thereof
resembling.

What inner torment must be
shorn into stripes?
Perhaps, some deranged internment
exorcised
of a holiday camp from Hell,
in an obscure resort,
along the coast, where
cut off
from the point, red flags
do not fly in warning
of a customary age
to stop sleeping with one's parents.

But beware,
such tribal markings,
in dark alleys,
if your nocturnal wanderings
take you there
and complimenting the truth
with reference
to a baboon's
most striking features:
they may not give a sporting chance,
before they bite.

❧ Check The Action ❧

Touch wood,
the tiger stripe is impervious
to ultra violet
glow and the shadow of the spotlight
glancing
off the sunburst's
flame.

Tell a tale of age
vaporizing
in the pink, then open
up the vintage case.

"Original?" is the standard question
marked up
from the source of 'origin', an undeclared
formality blending
smoothly in the walk-through.

Size up the '9'.
The drop dead gorgeous
figure
comes with strings
attached,
to pick the running order
of numbers, 'now secure'
under the lacquer's overspray.
But pluck the sweetest sounds, intently
from the air, with the price
redeemed
against a mortgage expectation.

One single cut
away from the headlines
of who fell down the stairs:

the burst-boy's landing
touches down,
to peg currency
and check the millimeter back-up
underneath the seat.

❧ Absolutely ❧

I am
the one, who is not,
to be petitioned.

I, too, have got the numbers,
of those who follow
the heaving crowds and believe
the proffered word.

Playback
the nightly sell outs
and monitor
the volume of outrage to the still
small voice
fading
from the master in the mix.

Contradiction is not a word
to entertain
in the role of the divine,
but through the medium of the applause
I confirm
your subscription cancelled
to the resurrection.

From the other side,
of curtain calls and the sirens
wailing,
the water of your baptism
rises steadily
above your ears.
Encore, you have finally
broken through.

❧ "I'm Your 'Lurve' Doctor, Baby." ❧

I. Respect

"Of course, I understand
the politics
you embrace, with your attachment
to the word.

Debate the meaning,
as I propose
the motion to undo
one button on your blouse
and stop

with my fingers
around the next."

ᴗᴗ II. A Second Opinion ᴗᴗ

He had not been caught
at it,
but what he caught, whilst
he was at it,
now laid him
lower
than his laid back practice
of unqualified license,
to culture each night's completed
course in good clean fun.

Adulterated
anti bodies trace the clinical
detachment,
in cases of referral.

A love bug, to test his patience
and resolve
to faithfully repeat,
as required
"Physician, heal thyself."

❧ Another Day At The Office ❧

He preferred his status, the acquiescent
poise of imperial immunity,
above the mundane reality of, " Honey,
I'm home,"
after a long day, cutting
through the red
tape of religious bureaucracy.

The roman guard, who didn't give a shit,
as they nailed their man
and exposed
His bodily functions to public scrutiny,
from a sanitary distance.

God dumped
the eternal stench of carcass and consummated
sin, load bearing
absolute, in its executed
set up, and liability
pre- eminent in the treatment
to willfully self destruct.

What augur of divine belief
was washed away,
in the charge of nationalistic fervor
and peace kill-cowed
at Pilates' public office of convenience?

His satrap's fingers indelibly
framed, within
the sacrificial bowl, now slopping
blood and water, beyond
the reaches of its sculpted porcelain
rim.

᷒ Saint Francis Re-appraised ᷒

With his arms outstretched, to receive
the birds, did Saint Francis
ever
doubt, in his contemplations
that he had got it wrong?

A fluttering of unease from his stomach
pit that betrayed
his uniqueness, through lack of courage,
or giving up to second best:
the tranquil landscape of the animals
friend, when the real need
was with the blood stained hands,
in the calling of the abattoir.

≈ Jump ≈

Why do I believe?

You take
all
and leave
nothing, but silence
calling

for me to follow
if my voice is not to be
extinguished.

Darkness trembles
in the slipstream
of the fall.

≈ The Plot Thickens ≈

It was nothing personal,
but personal business was
the gentle squeeze of compensation
in debit
to the calculated draft of the long range
drop,
from the mill tower's aerie scope.

A covert climb down of his steps
would still leave the ground
unbroken
and his reputation complete
in the clearance
above
suspicion, that a repeated load
had charged his mind.

He, alone
would see it coming,
the splintered veins of glass
concurring
with ballistic weight in flight.
One full stop, in punctuation
was neutral
to its ending, oblivious
to the fact,
or fiction.

SOFTLY, SOFTLY, THE LITERARY
CRITICS APPROACH ...

Beat The Critics

❧ A Poet's Self Critique ❧

Consistency of style and approach
elude him.
If he were a mugger,
one could rationalize with him,
confidently expecting him to hand over
his wallet.

What The Critics Said
(About Charles Measures Poetry)

"I had to make straight to the lavatory. I haven't been in so much pain for a long time. No wonder poetry begins with a capital 'P'.

—THE NETHER WALLOP GAZETTE.

"A Rock and Roll romantic, who has been caught in the middle of a head on collision for most of his life".

—THE MUSICAL EXCESS.

"We understand his work is perceived as a big job. We undertake to collect and knock the c..p out of it."

—COMPOST MAKER AND SEWAGE DISPOSAL DIGEST

"He writes books. I give right hooks. Both are HEAVY".

—GORGON - ART CRITIC
FOR GOTH WARRIOR PUBLICATIONS INC.

"This poet changes form to effect different voices, as guitar players change guitars to create different tonal textures. However, whilst some guitar players endeavour to say it all in one note, judging by the length of this book, the author has not conceived of the possibility of condensing it all into one word. For reader and poet alike one suggestion would be the word HELP!"

—HERMAN SHRINKS – EDITOR OF DAI- REOA
(DRASTICALLY AND INCISIVELY REDUCED ENCYCLOPEDIA OF AUTHORS)

"The poetry of someone who knows he might not make it back, but loses none of his ability to laugh as the cliff top draws ever nearer".

—THE NORTH FORELAND OBSERVER

"What book?"

—POETS' ANONYMOUS SOCIETY (P.A.S)

Notes

Groundsweat

Passing Bell -a bygone tradition of ringing the church bell the same number of times equal to the age of the person who had died.

Wake woman — a wake woman used to be found in rural areas acting as midwife, herbal specialist and as someone prepared to lay out the dead.

Wild West Stage

Shotguns and rifles were as prevalent in the Wild West as the legendary six shooters portrayed by Hollywood myth.

Bull barreled rifles were introduced in the 1830s as the first dedicated target rifle. Using smaller calibre bullets than other rifles, they had a range of 200 hundred yards. However, the older plains rifles in experienced hands could still find their target at 300 hundred yards.

Unquestioned

Until the 1970s, there were six boarding schools in Broadstairs, Kent, in close proximity to each other. Each school had an intake of approximately 100 children.

"San Francisco Calling"

1967 was the year of Flower Power and the arrival of Hippy culture promoting love and peace, with music being one of the main mediums.

Wong wong -the sound created by the wah-wah pedal on Jimi Hendrix's guitar from the track 'Burning Of The Midnight Lamp'. This was the first time that many people would have heard this sound effect on a recording.

The Stake

Haar -a Lincolnshire word meaning a deep sea mist. This term may have been introduced by the Danish invaders.

Domesticate Now

The film Apocalypse Now re-interpreted in the light of modern man discovering his feminine side.

Check The Action

The Action -the level of the guitar strings above the 12th fret.

A 'burst', or 'flame-top' -the nicknames for a 1959 Gibson Les Paul Standard (sunburst model) guitar. The Holy Grail of electric guitars. Caveat Emptor.

Absolutely.

If you go out live, for the record, you may be taken at your word and get what you ask for.

Roll The Credits

I would like to thank the following for all their support and encouragement, whilst I have been writing this book:

Richard "Hi Man!" Lawrence, who has been a stabilizing influence and listening ear throughout. Thank you especially for persevering beyond the call of duty with the great drawings, whilst I worked through the options of different titles and layouts, and also for transferring the final draft into a format ready for printing, which saved me taking a Dagenham screwdriver (a hammer) to my computer.

The Mole Valley Poets group and the Poetry Café group (from Walton on Thames) for the friendly atmosphere of their meetings, which became an important part of my creative focus.

Richard and Kelly West, Oli Harris, Michael and Margaret Farmery, Neil Davis and Dave Moyes (two of Australia's finest ambassadors), Lydia O'Brien, Bryn and Sally Howarth, and Phil Lloyd who all kindly looked at folders at various stages of completion.

Richard Chapman, who amazingly postponed his annual hibernation by a month, in order to read the final draft. Unfortunately, he fell asleep before I could get anything coherent from him. Never mind mate, I'll give you a wake up call next spring.

My wife Alison, who realized how important it was for me to write this book and very graciously allowed me the time and space to sit down and complete it.

During the production of this book, words were occasionally misspelt, verbs misconjulgated and the pages of dictionaries repeatedly turned over.

Index Of First Lines

Printed in the United Kingdom
by Lightning Source UK Ltd.
117005UKS00001B/316-549